CHRYSALIS
TAROT

9781572816893

Written by Toney Brooks
Paintings by Holly Sierra

Copyright © 2014 U.S. Games Systems, Inc.

All rights reserved. The illustrations, cover design and contents are protected by copyright. No part of this booklet may be reproduced in any form without permission in writing from the publisher, except by a reviewer who wishes to quote brief passages in connection with a review written for inclusion in a magazine, newspaper or website.

10 9

Made in China

Published by
U.S. Games Systems, Inc.
179 Ludlow Street, Stamford, CT 06902 USA
www.usgamesinc.com

INTRODUCTION

Tarot is about achieving your destiny; that co-creative, co-operative, maddening march through life filled with chance, chicanery and choice. The pursuit of personal destiny is a struggle to find inner peace, to find balance between an ego that wants and takes and a psyche that allows and gives.

By your side on your quest for self-fulfillment is an unseen force. It's an energy field known by many names and recognized by many masks; a force that informs your psyche and nudges you forward. In the Chrysalis Tarot, we refer to this force as the Otherworld.

In modern times, as tarot became associated with mysticism, divination and magic, users noticed the cards' uncanny ability to flesh out future possibilities. Tarot's illumination of your psyche is a vital component in the art of listening to your internal voice, raising self-awareness and informing decisions.

We invite you to browse through the Chrysalis Tarot cards. You'll find familiar and unfamiliar trump cards making up the Major Arcana. These 22 cards numbered 0 to 21 represent Otherworld characters and archetypes. Next up, the 40 Pip cards, numbered Ace through Ten in each suit, feature scenes that inspire personal reflection and stimulate your psychic intuition and imagination. The four suits that make up the Minor Arcana are: Stones (Pentacles); Mirrors (Cups); Spirals (Wands); and Scrolls (Swords).

Finally, you'll see we have replaced the traditional 16 Court cards with a fun-loving troupe of medieval troubadours. These merrymakers represent real-life messengers inspired by the Otherworld to assist you, especially at critical moments and troubling crossroads. Tarot invites questions, inspires the mind and whisks you on an adventurous journey within, a journey that is revealing, informative and fun. We trust it will be as fruitful as those journeys that led us to imagine and create this unique tarot deck.

THE MAJOR ARCANA

Traditionally in tarot the Major Arcana, or trump cards, are the deck's spiritual cards. Allow your Third Eye to study and reflect upon the images on the Chrysalis' Major Arcana cards. They convey different meanings to different people through their symbolism.

0 - MERLIN

Traditional Titles: FOOL or HERO
Attributes: NEW BEGINNINGS
  HEALING

Merlin's cuddly cat draws you at once into his mystery and magic. Cats, who have nine lives, symbolize rebirth, and nine indicates completion and perfection. Cats are forever curious and quick to take risks. While journeying into the unknown always involves risks, there are significant rewards for those willing to dive in deeply with an open mind.

Merlin's serpent-headed staff is a symbol of his power as a healer. The snake is a positive symbol indicating renewal and rebirth, the major theme of this card. In your reading, Merlin signifies innocence and potential. He constantly reminds you to let go of anxiety and preconceived notions about where you're going and how you'll get there. Approach your own hero's journey with a carefree attitude and have faith in Merlin's transforming magic. He will be constantly at your side as you explore Chrysalis Tarot.

I - RAVENS

Traditional Title: THE MAGICIAN
Attributes: SYNCHRONICITY
MESSENGER

The playful Chrysalis ravens make things happen. They play a game with pearls, which symbolize moonlight, mysticism and the magical phenomenon called synchronicity. The ravens, when not plotting mischief, perch in the upper branches—the spiritual realm—of the Tree of Life.

Ravens generate synchronicity in your life to help you become more mindful. The Ravens' message is to take care to see and catch these magic moments. The Ravens card in your reading is a heads-up to keep a good lookout for synchronicity—don't let it pass by unnoticed! Ravens also indicate you're now entering a new cycle in your life afresh with exciting possibilities.

II – SORCERESS

Traditional Title: THE HIGH PRIESTESS
Attributes: MYSTICISM
MAGIC

Sorceress Morgan Le Fay is pictured in vibrant hues of mysticism and magic. Her talisman represents the pomegranate, food of the Otherworld and a symbol of the Triple Goddess. We can feel the fruitful energy swirling in the background as it explodes in a crescendo of bursting light from Morgan's hand. Woven spirals symbolize the infinite transformative energy of the Sorceress.

In your reading, Morgan points to one of your more challenging encounters in attaining transformation. Morgan does her magic at the curtain that separates the seen and unseen worlds. The ravens, insatiably curious when magic is active, swoop in to flavor her cauldron with magical synchronicity, those coincidences that confirm you're on the right track.

III – GAIA

Traditional Title: THE EMPRESS
Attributes: NURTURING
ABUNDANCE

The ground we walk upon belongs to a holistic, conscious, self-regulating biosphere—a oneness we call Gaia, who sustains all life on Earth. Gaia is surrounded by the abundant beauty of her creation. She cradles a white dove, symbolic of peace, love and divinity. A nest filled with robin eggs represents birth and renewal. In your reading, Gaia symbolizes new ideas, new beginnings, new understandings, and sometimes even a new baby. This scene is flush with symbolism: the snail cautions you to be patient, the mouse to be trustful, and the lotus flower to be pure in heart.

Gaia is one of the Chrysalis cards honoring the Great Mother. When Gaia graces your reading she reminds you to be a positive, nurturing and loving person. By doing so, with her you will co-create your own abundance.

IV - GREEN MAN

Traditional Title: THE EMPEROR
Attributes: STRUCTURE
  NURTURING

Your inner voice is symbolized by Green Man's companion butterfly. It speaks to you in many meaningful ways through dreams, memory and intuition. This becomes apparent in readings where Green Man appears, so pay close attention to surrounding cards. As Gaia's spiritual consort, Green Man reigns with the Sun card as a patriarch and judicious father figure. Green Man's constant refrain is harmonious coexistence, balance and structure. Count on him to reveal unexpected signs in nature to validate your dreams, memories and intuition. His unmatched imaginative energy inspires you to ever-greater accomplishments.

V – DIVINE CHILD

Traditional Title: THE HIEROPHANT
Attribute: SELF-DISCOVERY

The Divine Child archetype symbolizes your full potential. The child, male or female, is surrounded by reminders of transformation, such as the butterflies and frog. The colors on the palette represent emotions and choices. The scallop shell design represents the many pathways a pilgrim takes in search of enlightenment. They all lead to inner light, divinity and self-discovery, symbolized by a single candle.

Most tarot decks title this card the Hierophant, a religious authority figure. In Chrysalis Tarot, the task of spiritual growth is an individual responsibility that requires an open mind and critical thinking. When Divine Child lights up your reading, you are asked to embrace yourself. Self-acceptance through self-discovery is the way of the seeker and the pathway to destiny.

VI – LOVERS

Traditional Title: THE LOVERS
Attributes: UNITY
ONENESS

Joyful forest animals gather around a Celtic marriage ceremony beside the Tree of Life. The Lovers card evokes the union of opposites through the natural energy of mutual attraction. This celebration of Oneness is animated by spiritual energy and great expectation.

When the Lovers card appears in your reading, it may or may not have to do with a wedding. The Lovers can also symbolize the reconciliation of conflicting values or beliefs. Whether this reconciliation involves romantic love or your worldview, this card anticipates a significant leap forward. When Lovers appear in your reading, the irrepressible drive that moves you to bite the forbidden apple and exit the garden of delusion takes command.

VII – HERNE THE HUNTER

Traditional Title: THE CHARIOT
Attributes: FOCUS
DIVINE ASSISTANCE

The mighty Herne leads his wild hunt through the countryside and dense forest amid the clamor of baying hounds, braying horses and the screeching winds of a fierce winter storm. He symbolizes the dogged might of your willpower to overcome obstacles. Herne's helmet sports the majestic horns of the red stag, Lord of the Forest. Three stars of Orion's Belt above his head represent the three Celestial Personages who tend the gateway to higher consciousness.

Herne's presence in your reading foretells success, and offers affirmative response to any specific query you presented to the cards.

VIII – MA'AT

Traditional Titles: JUSTICE
Attribute: BALANCE

Ma'at, the Egyptian goddess of justice, truth and order, holds creation in equilibrium to prevent a return to primeval chaos. Her wings spread the promise of motherly protection and love throughout your reading. Ma'at's primary symbol is an ostrich feather, which represents truth. Her lioness companion is named Sekhmet, Lioness of the Sun. In ancient Egypt, the lotus flower of rebirth was Sekhmet's personal symbol. She protects the righteous and destroys the wicked. Like a stalking lioness, Sekhmet reminds you to take a cautious, deliberate approach to problems. Ma'at warns you to harness your impulsive ego and not allow it to push you headfirst into poor choices. Sekhmet's energy assures you that thoughtfulness and balance will prevail.

IX - STORYTELLER

Traditional Title: THE HERMIT
Attributes: WISDOM
  CONTEMPLATION

The Storyteller appears in your reading to announce an opportunity for introspection. She cradles her sacred healing orb, the symbol of a life examined. A pair of orioles denotes her shape-shifting abilities and mystical connection to distant realms. A crown of ferns at her brow assures you of sincerity and friendship.

Storyteller asks you to confide in her. She invites you to elevate your apprehensions, secrets and desires to full conscious awareness. When Storyteller appears in your reading, it means the time is favorable for quiet solitude. Her meditation mandalas can turn your dreams into reality.

X - WHEEL

Traditional Title: THE WHEEL OF FORTUNE
Attribute: CONSEQUENCE

The Wheel emerges from the Tree of Life, reminding you that life resembles a game of chance. The devotional figurine is Fortuna, goddess of fate and luck. Attaining destiny, Wheel's highest desire for you involves life cycles of action and consequence. The Wheel asks you to recall experiences that at the time seemed insignificant, but in hindsight reveal a path that eventually led to some greater purpose. Such mysteries illuminate the meaning and the power of the Wheel. In your reading, the Wheel suggests that you've arrived at a critical juncture in the present cycle. The Wheel, Fortuna and aromatic sage wafting from the smudging pot remind you that you control your life through the choices you make.

XI – PAPA LEGBA

Traditional Title: STRENGTH
Attribute: INNER STRENGTH

Papa Legba wiles away his time on a stone wall in the middle of the 22 Major Arcana. He stands between you and destiny's pathway higher up on the ridge. Two candles, an unusual staff, and handy knapsack indicate he is master of the mystical gateway between your subconscious mind and the Otherworld. Summoned by drumbeats of spiritual wakefulness, Papa navigates your Chrysalis exploration of the unseen world. He reminds you that inner strength and self-control are required to attain higher consciousness.

In your reading, Papa draws attention to desires that may pose a conflict to personal destiny and self-fulfillment. The transforming energy of Papa Legba, depicted by the engraving on the rock wall, asks you to let go and surrender your ego to the guidance found in this reading.

XII - CELTIC OWL

Traditional Title: THE HANGED MAN
Attribute: REBIRTH

Celtic Owl urges you to seek out wisdom and open your mind to new ways of thinking. The interwoven Celtic knot reminds you to be mindful of the intricacies and connectivity of all creation. The unseen world remains dark to many because its reality is doubted or denied. An owl has the ability to see clearly in the black of night. Against starry skies, Celtic Owl symbolizes seeing creation holistically and suggests this as a personal goal to consider. However, this goal cannot be achieved quickly; it requires patience, imagination and frequent contemplation. Only if you embrace the divine light can Celtic Owl help you attain the harmony, peace and transformation taught by all the great sages.

> Celtic Owl artwork was inspired in part by a nature photograph taken by John Hendrickson.

XIII – ARIADNE

Traditional Title: DEATH
Attribute: TRANSFORMATION

This card takes you to the center of Ariadne's labyrinth where you'll meet the dreaded Minotaur. Ariadne, Celtic goddess of the gates of time, offers you a spool of yarn to unwind as you proceed so you can safely trace your way out of the labyrinth. The Minotaur symbolizes your shadow-side, the part of your psyche where negative thoughts lurk alongside repressed feelings such as anger, guilt and selfishness. You successfully slay the metaphorical Minotaur and free yourself when you take full ownership of these flaws and grant unconditional forgiveness to others. The presence of Ariadne in your reading suggests that you assist a friend or loved one in finding his own way out of a dark corner.

XIV – GOLDEN FLOWER

Traditional Title: TEMPERANCE
Attributes: HARMONY
                    MEDITATION

Golden Flower's sunburst mandala prompts you to meditate upon the natural ebb and flow of life's ups and downs. The fish portray active restoration of balance through appreciation and acceptance, as opposed to resistance and resignation. The butterflies symbolize Golden Flower's energy radiating outward as evolving consciousness.

The Major Arcana archetypes in Chrysalis Tarot are the emanations of eons of human history, memory and experience accessible to the conscious mind through active meditation. In your reading, Golden Flower means you are drawing nearer to conscious awareness.

XV – BELLA ROSA

Traditional Title: THE DEVIL
Attribute: DETACHMENT

Mystical Bella Rosa struts through Carnevale de Venezia attired in safe anonymity. Her persona is a fabrication symbolized by her mask, a projection of who she really is deep down inside.

Most of us behave similarly and doing so is healthy, unless you permit yourself to over-identify with a false persona. Bella Rosa assures you that it's okay to be yourself. Bella Rosa clutches her looking glass, a symbol of self-indulgence and a narcissistic ego. Her red rose symbolizes detachment. Bella Rosa is about understanding the benefit of detachment from material obsessions and unhealthy habits. The encouraging

Ouroboros symbol (a snake eating its own tail) indicates rebirth and fulfillment of a cycle.

XVI – KALI

Traditional Title: THE TOWER
Attribute: CREATIVE DESTRUCTION

Kali personifies the cleansing energy of creative destruction as she restores balance to your life. This card indicates you may be stubbornly clinging to something or someone, a mindset or worldview that is incompatible with your quest for self-fulfillment. Therefore, your challenge is to deconstruct this physical or mental architecture, whatever it may be, and move forward.

Some find that forging new paths and altering circumstances is daunting. Kali beckons your cooperation in restoring harmony and balance. The skulls, which are positive symbols, signify transition to an evolved state of being. The lightning flashes from her tongue are verbal calls to action.

XVII – ELPI

Traditional Title: THE STAR
Attributes: HOPE
                    CHOICES

Each evening when the sun sets, Elpi, whose name means hope, lights her Golden Censor and prepares to dash across the sky. With help from four steeds, which symbolize the four winds, she sets the darkened skies ablaze with fiery lights to symbolize the good things that got away.

When Pandora opened her mythological box, a swarm of evil escaped into the world. Hope was the only good thing that remained behind. Elpi is that promise of hope and brighter days. She reminds you never to despair as you confront life's inevitable misfortunes. Elpi reminds you that the choices you make today determine your future, and always to visualize destiny bathed in hopeful starlight.

XVIII – MOON

Traditional Title: THE MOON
Attribute: REFLECTION

A surrealistic dreamscape invites you to drift into the depths of your subconscious mind. The bejeweled crescent moon is crowned with an eight-pointed star. She embraces the tiny island as a mother might embrace a bewildered child. The Moon calls you to creative reflection. Her mysteries will be revealed in due course when you least expect them. If you feel stranded and bewildered, energize your goals and aspirations with positive thoughts. The Moon is about the joyful celebration of your success. An encounter with the Moon is an encounter with the Great Mother, who asks you to listen attentively to your inner voice, dreams and intuition. They have amazing power to alter your future.

XIX – SUN

Traditional Title: THE SUN
Attribute: EMPOWERMENT

In a moment of tenderness, Sun sheds a fatherly tear because so many of his children neglect beauty, truth and justice in favor of materialism, power and dogma. Yet even a lamenting Sun is an excellent card to have in your reading. In addition to brightening your day with boundless optimism, Sun empowers you to see your endeavors to successful conclusions. The Sun symbolizes enlightenment, which is depicted as conscious awareness flowing in eight directions. The Sun and Moon inspire you to take a break from your busy routine and reconnect with nature.

XX – PHOENIX

Traditional Title: JUDGMENT
Attribute: RESOLUTION

The mythological Phoenix rises brilliantly from the fire and ashes of creative destruction. This archetype is about lessons learned, order restored and the dawn of a new day. This is always a welcome card to see in your reading. Phoenix calls your attention to the energies of consciousness flowing from the Otherworld. Phoenix's radiant colors indicate high energies of inspirational consciousness stirring in your life. This card heralds a time of resolution and restoration; a time to reap rewards and trust your instincts and intuition.

XXI - PSYCHE

Traditional Title: THE WORLD
Attribute: ASCENSION

Psyche dances onto the world stage to herald your glorious success. This card is about those moments of clarity that bring quantum leaps of awareness and understanding. Transformation is a lifelong work in progress, a continuing quest for renewal and growth. When one growth cycle ends another begins. You travel through many doorways on the quest for fulfillment. Psyche's message is to mind the thresholds lest you become stuck in the certitude of absolutes and cease to grow. *Psyche* translates as either soul or butterfly in Greek. As a beautiful butterfly, Psyche symbolizes the transformation of consciousness called ascension, your highest calling.

THE MINOR ARCANA

The 40 cards numbered Ace through 10 are called Pips and can be thought of as tarot's consciousness cards. The various characteristics of the Pips provide the mortar that binds your reading into a coherent whole. The Pips encourage you to employ your own creativity and intuition and infer the cards' deeper meaning while being guided by the keywords and artistic symbolism.

THE SUIT OF STONES

Traditional Names: PENTACLES or COINS
Values: HAPPINESS
PROSPERITY

Stones represent the element of Earth, matter and material consciousness. The suit's highest values are material happiness and prosperity. Stones help you identify specific material or physical values exerting influence upon your reading: values that can be desirable or undesirable.

ACE of STONES
Keyword: ABUNDANCE

The Ace of Stones depicts a sacred megalith like those found in Stone Age circles located in many parts of the world. The Ace of Stones reaches into the morning sky warmed by brush strokes of soft sunlight heralding the beginning of a new day or cycle. The sacred stone appears as an outcrop on a hillock covered by lush, spring flora. It's a scene bristling with the energies of fresh beginnings and the promises of endless possibilities. In your reading, this very positive, affirming card indicates abundance. You can expect to attain your immediate goals with thoughtful planning and flexibility.

TWO of STONES
Keyword: TRUST

The King of the Forest reminds you to maintain your balance and trust your next step. Sheaths of windswept ice in this scene give way to rippling, clear waters as winter gives way to springtime. This card is about trusting and cooperating with emerging energies. When the season changes, the bear emerges from hibernation, and the once frozen lake bubbles anew with life. In your reading, this card tells you to balance contrasting energies and to remain firmly grounded, sure-footed and secure like the mighty bear.

THREE of STONES
Keyword: PLANNING

The Three of Stones card signifies a culmination of your efforts: your planning, hard work and dedication have paid off. But the journey continues. What hidden surprises await you as the trilithon chamber beckons you hither? The triquetras on the upright stones symbolize protection. The comforting campfire invites you to approach the Tree of Life's hidden realm. The owls are named Strength, Growth and Interconnectedness. This card affirms that you've hit on the right plan and should carry forward.

FOUR of STONES
Keyword: POSSESSIONS

An ornately bejeweled chest filled with your most prized possessions blocks the pathway to self-understanding. This card might be a warning not to overvalue material things. Or, it could signal that you've become reticent to making needed changes in your life. The Four of Stones is frequently presented as a card fraught with troubles, but as with most things, proper balance is key. While the Four of Stones acknowledges your accomplishments to date, now may be an ideal time to slide the chest to one side and consider the higher matters of life.

FIVE of STONES
Keyword: DESOLATION

Cards numbered five in tarot usually point to a misfortune or hardship to overcome. With the Five of Stones, this misfortune is often material or financial. Desolation, however, might also be the result of loneliness or isolation, as depicted on this card. The most encouraging symbol on the Five of Stones is the wild cherry tree, which signifies renewal, regeneration, a fresh start or improved outlook. This card is the silver lining to the clouds of hardship everyone endures.

SIX of STONES
Keyword: CARITAS

Six talismans carved from beryl gemstones swing from the Tree of Life. The green ones are emeralds; the gold ones are called heliodors or "Gifts of the Sun." This card is about giving and receiving. The green and gold talismans symbolize *caritas*—charity of love for others and charity of love for self. The Tree of Life's interwoven energy flows upward from its roots to nurture personal growth and self-understanding.

In your reading, this card draws your attention to charity, empathy and acceptance of others.

SEVEN of STONES
Keyword: REGRET

Meditating beside an ancient stone arch, the maiden Syrinx reflects on her choices and the rewards they may bring. This pastoral scene above the sacred River Ladon winds a thread of hope through the lush valley below. Surely the river will wash away the maiden's regret just as it healed Demeter, whose red poppies confirm that the Seven of Stones is about healing. Even if the result of recent actions produced the desired effect, a vague sense of regret may still linger. Follow Demeter's example and toss regret and sorrow into the river, and get on with life.

EIGHT of STONES
Keyword: INGENUITY

Stonehenge is a living testament to the ingenuity of the ancients. This inviting scene is alive with a flurry of pictograms, including one of the red deer. His antlers were used to make picks to unearth the foundations for these huge stones. Other tools and a clay crucible symbolize the end of Stone Age technology. Accordingly, this card says a new and exciting change is on your horizon. An encouraging card to have, the Eight of Stones suggests a successful endeavor may be nearing its conclusion, and that now's a good time to think about your transition.

NINE of STONES
Keyword: INDIFFERENCE

A meticulously ordered group of nine stones represents the well-earned accomplishments of hard work and diligence. This maiden has realized there's more to life than security and material possessions. Her decision set in stone, she confidently turns her back to the old and sets her sights on a brave new adventure. Her shaman's walking stick symbolizes cosmic connection between the worlds. It also symbolizes authority as she lets go and takes control of her own life. The Nine of Stones is about taking stock from time to time, weighing options carefully and being willing to take risks.

TEN of STONES
Keyword: POSSESSIVE

Woe to the soul who attempts to wrestle away this sprite's prized possessions that he worked so hard for. This sprite has become entwined in an aggressive and possessive overgrowth of vines, a negative representation of worldly ties that bind. These Gordian knots define who he is and, unless he detaches himself psychologically, threaten to stymie personal growth and his physical well-being. The Ten of Stones is about healthy choices to prioritize your success in the material world. Tarot cards numbered ten signify transition to the next growth cycle once your priorities are balanced.

THE SUIT of MIRRORS

Traditional Name: CUPS
Values: NOURISHMENT
                    LOVE

Mirrors represent the element of Water and introspective consciousness. The specific attributes of Mirrors are feelings and emotions. The suit's highest values are nourishment and love. The Mirror pips accentuate the values of self-examination and self-awareness.

ACE of MIRRORS
Keyword: FEELINGS

As with all aces, the Ace of Mirrors heralds a new beginning. While the suit of Stones navigates the physical realm, the suit of Mirrors reflects the watery currents of feelings and the tides of human emotion. On this card you meet Daphne, a water nymph and daughter of Gaia. The Ace of Mirrors means either new romantic love, symbolized by the two candles, or a steady flow of creative energy. The turtle knows good fortune both in water and on land. The sea plants to either side of Daphne symbolize subterranean energy influencing a new project.

TWO of MIRRORS
Keyword: UNION

The Two of Mirrors card is concerned with union, beauty and partnership. Two snuggling swans proclaim everlasting love and bring a joyful message of mutual commitment. They foretell a new romance, a budding business partnership or a new, enduring friendship. The union of two hearts brings promise of loyalty and mutual respect. The swans' matching mirrors are reminders to project positive energy so it can reflect back upon you.

THREE of MIRRORS
Keyword: COMPASSION

The Three of Mirrors is about coming together in joyful celebration with family and friends. The lion and lamb symbolize a harmonious sense of self-acceptance we must discover and nurture within our own hearts before we are capable of extending compassion to others.

The implicit message of the Three of Mirrors in your reading is Do No Harm. This is a card that exudes happiness and optimism. It bodes new romance, creative new ventures or simply a joyful occasion to see yourself reflected in the mirrors of love, compassion and good fortune.

FOUR of MIRRORS
Keyword: DETACHMENT

Daphne the water nymph has shape-shifted into an alluring mermaid. The four mirrors symbolize security and stability. When at her emotional best, she's empathetic and nurturing in relationships. When at her human worst, however, she becomes detached, neglectful or even mean. This occurs when overwrought emotions hold sway, a condition spawning self-indulgent behavior. In your reading, this card cautions you not to unintentionally sabotage your relationships.

FIVE of MIRRORS
Keyword: FORGIVENESS

This card is about overcoming disenchantment and gaining healing through forgiveness. In your reading, the Five of Mirrors may signify a broken romance or some difficult emotional upheaval that needs to be set right. For guidance, your eyes turn to Quan Yin, who rises sublimely from a five-mirror lotus flower. Quan Yin's story is one of hope from the depths of adversity, joy from the depths of sorrow, and justification from the depths of deceit. Whatever wrongs you may have suffered will heal with time. But wounds heal faster and bear fewer scars when you grant gifts of mercy and compassion to those who have wronged you.

SIX of MIRRORS
Keyword: MEMORIES

This delightful chap is an Irish sidhe, a child-like, fun-loving nature spirit who is particularly fond of flowers, music and water. This card is about fanciful flights of memory, as symbolized by the six reflecting pools. Each pool reflects memories from different time periods. The Six of Mirrors indicates, for better or worse, energy patterns that affect the present and perhaps mold your future. This card points to unseen activities that rely upon your maintaining balance and harmony in your life.

SEVEN of MIRRORS
Keyword: DISCERNMENT

The Lady of Shalott spends day in and day out isolated in her tower chamber. For her, the reality of the outside world is trapped in seven mirrors. This leaves her confused and unsatisfied, if not tormented, by the fleeting illusions she must weave into her tapestry of destiny. The Seven of Mirrors is about discernment, false reality and free will. A crystalline vessel symbolizing purity reminds you to keep a firm grip on what is real and what is illusion when making important decisions. Although you may feel confused or conflicted, the time draws nigh to weigh options and make your choice.

EIGHT of MIRRORS
Keyword: SELFLESS

Celtic Vates, like the one pictured on the Eight of Mirrors, are Druid prophets who concern themselves with life's higher mysteries. This Vate follows Arianrhod, the Moon Goddess of the Silver Wheel who hails from the Isle of Avalon. She is depicted on his walking stick as a symbol of wisdom and fate. In your reading, the Eight of Mirrors card urges you to pursue the words of the prophets written on the mountainsides of self-awareness. The eight mirrors lining the sacred path reflect the teachings of the great sages: selflessness, truthfulness, harmlessness, mindfulness, respectfulness, goodness, peacefulness and righteousness.

NINE of MIRRORS
Keyword: JOY

The Nine of Mirrors radiates the vibrational energy of Quan Yin's Golden Flower. The Flower's genies have been let out of their vases and now joyfully frolic in the Tree of Life. They invite you to make a wish—the Nine of Mirrors is Chrysalis Tarot's wish card! Raindrops are falling everywhere, bringing peace, balance and harmony upon all areas of your life. It also tells you to pay special attention to the meaning of nearby Major Arcana cards.

TEN OF MIRRORS
Keyword: PEACE

The rainbow dove of peace ferries ten pretty mirrors that represent an emerging new cycle for you, as well as emotional fulfillment in the present cycle. The Ten of Mirrors is one of the most positive cards in the Chrysalis deck. It signals contentment and joy and may allude to marriage, enduring friendship or the thrill of a new adventure.

This card is about just letting things be. Very little effort on your part is required now. Trying to control a romantic situation could send it afoul. The Ten of Mirrors indicates you've attained a significant goal and are well prepared when opportunity knocks.

THE SUIT OF SPIRALS

Traditional Name: WANDS
Values: PASSION
PERSONAL GROWTH

The Chrysalis Tarot Spirals represent rational thinking and the element of Fire. The specific attribute of the Suit of Spirals is Energy. The suit's highest values are passion and personal growth.

ACE of SPIRALS
Keyword: ENERGY

The raw power and energy of the proud Aries ram introduces the Suit of Spirals. Like all tarot Aces, this too is a positive, growth-oriented card. The feathers symbolize accomplishments of your imagination as well as a spiritual renaissance. The iridescent peacock feather is a sign of transformation. All Aces represent seeds that must be nourished physically, emotionally and spiritually to reach full potential. The Ace of Spirals symbolizes the energy of mental nourishment: new ideas, fresh inspirations and stimulating opportunities. This card indicates that it is an ideal time for setting goals.

TWO of SPIRALS
Keyword: CHOICE

This card is about making choices and planning ahead just as this little bird is doing. The Two of Spirals cautions that all information needed to make an informed decision may not yet be apparent. The bird feeds her instinctive creative energies while patiently discerning between her choices, depicted by contrasting patterns of spiraling energy. Our clever mother-to-be chose to build in a mulberry tree, a symbol of wisdom and patience. The Two of Spirals tells you to weigh pros and cons carefully in the matters before you. Then, be patient and choose wisely.

THREE of SPIRALS
Keyword: CONTEMPLATION

This card arouses a thoughtful Cambodian monk from his meditation. He senses a helping hand may be required to move a project along to successful completion. This card's energy is self-expressive, so final decisions are yours alone to make. However, the Three of Spirals is about maintaining an open mind and entertaining the helpful counsel of others. Active contemplation assists your decision making by producing crystalline energy that clears your head. This card reminds you that the rigors of everyday life may sap your energy, and urges you to slow things down.

FOUR of SPIRALS
Keyword: SOLITUDE

The emerging energy of the Four of Spirals suggests it's time for peaceful solitude and introspection. This heralds an opportunity to regather and recharge by changing your perspective. The waxing crescent moon indicates that it's a good time to clean the interior of your

Harvest Home, as the broom loudly suggests. Clearly, this card says you need to sweep something away.

The Four of Spirals is also about relaxing to enjoy the fruits of your labor and life's great rewards. Visualize yourself observing a new world of possibilities from the upper floor picture window. It's a new season and a fresh challenge is on the horizon.

FIVE of SPIRALS
Keyword: SHADOW

A mighty dragon hurls the conflicting energies of fiery spirals deep into crevasses of your subconscious mind. These fireballs cast shadows representing repressed feelings of resentment, unhealthy desires and self-centeredness or greed.

The twelve-petal lotus mandala depicted on the dragon's wing provides an inviting focal point for contemplation. The Five of Spirals in your reading asks you to shine the light of conscious awareness on your own shadows and subdue them. Struggles customarily associated with this card are interior conflicts. With effort and diligence you'll vanquish any dragons that haunt you.

SIX of SPIRALS
Keyword: SUCCESS

In the light of a full moon, six unfurled clooties sway from a sacred hawthorn tree. The Celts tied bits of cloth called clooties on trees near springs and wells where nature spirits dwell as votive offerings. The practice continues today. Clooties have come to symbolize wishes fulfilled.

In your reading, the Six of Spirals spells success. Persistence has paid off, a goal was accomplished, a wish was granted. Now the hawthorn tree symbolizes transition—the shedding of leaves to make way for new growth. If you hoped for a positive sign, the Six of Spirals could be it!

SEVEN of SPIRALS
Keyword: ASSERTION

A well-rested bear focuses his piercing gaze on an unnamed intruder. The Seven of Spirals is about assertion and defending your turf. Turf can be a metaphor for your business, your personal beliefs or even your right as an adult simply to exercise your own free will.

The bear symbolizes the inner strength and confidence required to assert yourself with authority. The meaning of the Seven of Spirals is to stand firm while holding overwrought emotions in check. Be tenacious and unyielding like the bear and you will prevail.

EIGHT of SPIRALS
Keyword: ANSWERS

A red stag leaps majestically through the dense thicket surrounding his magical forest. A Hunter's Moon tells you his instincts and intuition are piqued to their highest vibration. The Eight of Spirals is about swift progress and receipt of long sought answers, symbolized by shooting stars.

The Eight of Spirals bodes well for rapid progress and successful conclusion of unresolved matters. The Hunter's Moon, also known as the Blood Moon, marks a time when ancestral energy from the Otherworld reaches its highest peak. In your reading, this card says to pay attention to random thoughts and peculiar dreams.

NINE of SPIRALS
Keyword: PERSEVERANCE

The ancient wind-blower Aeolus, Captain of the Four Winds, sends gently spiraling winds in your direction when the Nine of Spirals unfurls. The circling ravens symbolize the cardinal winds: north, south, east and west, which represent energies of change. Wind is the great cosmic organizer. The Nine of Spirals is about holding fast to your course and shaping creative solutions when ill winds blow. Like all tarot cards numbered nine, this card signals completion of your efforts and success.

TEN of SPIRALS
Keyword: CROSSROADS

Oh, to be fully human! This centaur is sometimes ruled by his human heart, other times by his base instincts. Bound up bundles of negative energy symbolize his past regrets, missed opportunities and unbecoming behavior—an unbearable burden. He arrives at a crossroads, the ultimate symbol for life-changing choice. The Ten of Spirals in your reading is a cue to improve your energy and lighten your load. Draw the reins in on the difficult cycle this card signifies and choose the high road. This card says, "Don't play the blame game; put the past behind you and don't look back."

SUIT OF SCROLLS

Traditional Name: SWORDS
Values: INTUITION
CLARITY

Scrolls represent the element of Air and the intellect. The specific attribute of the Suit of Scrolls is Intuition, which is the suit's highest value. Scrolls are truth-bearing cards pointing to clarity of thought.

ACE of SCROLLS
Keyword: INTUITION

A wise raven perches on a parchment scroll where knowledge of the higher things in life is written. Nearby keys symbolize abundant energy and raw potential to be unlocked. The Ace of Scrolls heralds a creative impulse to be nurtured through expansion of your mind, as symbolized by the bending tree remaining tall in the face of adversity. Unlocking energy powerful enough to change the way you see things brings mental conflict. Complacent souls may actively oppose you. This Ace says stand fast. Sheer determination and the will to succeed assure your victory.

TWO of SCROLLS
Keyword: FANTASY

A winged, black unicorn is a rare sight indeed. She symbolizes immense, swift power and contradiction. This card is about facing difficult choices and trusting your instincts. But first it reminds you to order your life and maintain perspective. A particular dilemma you face could require a flight of fantasy. Avoid the tendency to overthink a complex problem. By taking a fantastical, imaginative, even impractical approach, you may hit upon a practical solution. The unicorn's horn signifies the sword of counterintuitive thinking that penetrates the highest realms of wisdom.

THREE of SCROLLS
Keyword: REJECTION

The Three of Scrolls is about the pain of letting go. Our sorrowful fox sheds purple teardrops of emancipation and freedom. Newfound freedom is often accompanied by painful feelings such as rejection, betrayal or broken promises. Times of difficulty and sadness are like violent emotional thunderstorms. Once they pass, rainbows appear. The Three of Scrolls asks you to visualize a rainbow's violet band of light. This color vibration connects you to the Otherworld's unseen purposes. For a time, such purposes may remain concealed like the wily fox. But they are there nonetheless, so be patient and stay positive.

FOUR of SCROLLS
Keyword: RECOLLECTION

The colorful wings on the Four of Scrolls indicate that this is a period of healing. It's a time to be alone with your thoughts to plan and visualize your future and to place the past aside. Hopeful butterfly wings symbolize transformation and self-fulfillment through self-acceptance. Only when we fully accept who we are can we accept others as they are. In your reading, the Four of Scrolls tells you to draw your energies close so you may experience inner peace and tranquility during this time of healing and acceptance.

FIVE of SCROLLS
Keyword: SACRIFICE

The Five of Scrolls is about sacrifice and victory. The sword plunged into stone represents the hard realities of the world. Excalibur has affixed these Scrolls of Higher Consciousness to the great symbol of the material world where it awaits your honorable sacrifice of righteousness. The sword of sacrifice can be extracted in different ways. The Five of Scrolls may ask you to focus more on the needs of others at this time than on your own. It may caution you to fight off gathering clouds of negative energy. It may ask for the sacrifice of higher consciousness over petty concerns and selfish trivialities.

SIX of SCROLLS
Keyword: CONSOLATION

The Six of Scrolls is about removing obstacles to higher learning, an attribute shared with Ganesha, the elephant-headed Hindu deity. It also relates to consolation experienced as peace, balance and harmony. The small scroll held by the elephant implies that only a little work remains in your present cycle. The new cycle awaiting your energy and inspiration will be one of learning and wisdom. The larger scrolls might include a map indicating future travel. This card's advice is to be open and adaptable.

SEVEN of SCROLLS
Keyword: INDECISION

This young satyr is perplexed. He holds a single scroll symbolizing all the knowledge and rationale he can muster. He is inclined to choose the door on the left as the door on the right appears risky. The Six of Scrolls' counterintuitive reasoning is symbolized by a single scroll.

The Seven of Scrolls asks you to take risks and allow your counterintuitive reasoning to hold sway. Many courageous decisions are made just because they feel right.

EIGHT of SCROLLS
Keyword: ILLUSION

The Eight of Scrolls is about dealing with conflict and illusions of the senses. Our Egyptian visionary will help you sort out your problems by reading her eight scrolls. You may sometimes find yourself caught up in whirlwinds of your own making. But there's good news! In your reading, these scrolls promise a positive outcome. The Eight of Scrolls asks you to be introspective and rid yourself of self-serving illusions. Reframe issues and visualize positive, creative outcomes. This card simply says "Stop worrying." Consider seeking out others for sage advice.

NINE of SCROLLS
Keyword: DESPAIR

The Nine of Scrolls illustrates despair and anguish brought about by subconsciously entombed aspects of the personality. This angelic messenger, symbolizing trauma, is exhausted from dealing with a difficult hurdle before you're able to complete an important growth cycle.

In your reading, the Nine of Scrolls means you're struggling with overblown fears. Upon introspection, you may find you're projecting long repressed issues onto friends and family. Nightmares can result from buried guilt, regret and other emotional baggage. The turmoil will dissipate as you assume greater responsibility for your own well-being.

TEN of SCROLLS
Keyword: EXILE

Tiger energy representing a reversal of fortune is imprisoned by the Ten of Scrolls. Our somewhat bewildered tiger is held captive by a negative cycle related to an important lesson. This lesson needs to be learned before the cycle can end. Until then, it simply goes on repeating itself.

The Ten of Scrolls is about recognizing undesirable, repeating patterns in your life. Such patterns are usually fueled by negativity. In other words, negative behavior is like a magnet that attracts itself. The passionate energy of the tiger overcomes unlearned lessons. Tiger energy is strong-willed, confident and resolved.

THE TROUPE

The Chrysalis Troupe is a delightful ensemble of medieval merrymakers. Unlike archetypes, the Troupe's characters stand in for real-world people and personality types from your past, present or future. They may be family, friends, acquaintances or even total strangers. You attract them naturally via compatible energy signatures. Using synchronicity, the Otherworld places these characters in your path to be mentors, messengers, mystics and muses.

This much is true with all spiritual quests: you never walk alone. We humans are interdependent; you meet those who you are destined to meet. Our Troupe corresponds to traditional tarot Court cards. There's an equal number of male and female characters in the Chrysalis Tarot Troupe. However, in real life these characters may appear as men or women of any age.

THE MINSTREL

Traditional Name: KING of PENTACLES
KING of STONES
Attributes: ASSERTIVE
LOYAL
Role: MENTOR

As your official or unofficial financial advisor, the Minstrel is a reliable source of knowledge. Often a relative or trusted friend, occasionally a professional, he tethers you to reality. The Minstrel is your confidante in money matters. Like his canine companion, he's loyal and reassuring, and is someone who knows you well. In your reading, the Minstrel's cheerful tune confirms financial or physical well-being or both.

THE ARTISTE

Traditional Name: QUEEN of PENTACLES
QUEEN of STONES
Attributes: SPIRITUAL
MAGNETIC
Role: MUSE

The Artiste paints your path through a tranquil grove of ash trees. A butterfly watches the process of transforming blank canvas into glorious reality, a metaphor for your personal journey.

The multi-talented Artiste imparts prophetic

wisdom to others without realizing it. She is a gentle, soft-spoken person sent to inspire you through art, dance, music and poetry. You'll find yourself immediately drawn to her as she charts your progress with brush strokes of wise and sensible advice.

THE ILLUSIONIST

Traditional Name: KNIGHT of PENTACLES
 KNIGHT of STONES
Attributes: SPONTANEOUS
 CONFUSING
Role: MYSTIC

The Illusionist is an unusual person filled with youthful exuberance—perhaps a gifted Indigo Child. Throughout the ages, illusionists have been mythology's tricksters and this person certainly is no exception. In real life, tricksters are simply misunderstood mystics.

The Illusionist appears in your reading to spur you to action without a lot of confusing forethought. If you're up for risky, raw adventure, follow his lead without reservation. "Nothing ventured, nothing gained," says the Illusionist.

THE ACROBAT

Traditional Name:	PAGE of PENTACLES
	PAGE of STONES
Attributes:	TRANSITION
	PERSPECTIVE
Role:	MESSENGER

When you meet the Acrobat, she'll inspire you to rise above your troubles and vault up to a fresh reality. She invites you to appreciate that there's always more than one way to see things. This card is about gaining perspective.

Her playful primate symbolizes the mobility of thought that comes through learning. The Acrobat is a studious, serious person with a frolicsome sense of humor. In your reading, she promises good news and unexpected developments.

THE SOJOURNER

Traditional Name:	KING of CUPS
	KING of MIRRORS
Attributes:	EMPATHETIC
	WISE
Role:	MENTOR

The Sojourner is one of the most interesting individuals you will encounter. He is good-natured, emotionally balanced, and filled with wisdom and empathy. The Sojourner is the Troupe's foremost mentor because he's remarkably insightful.

The Sojourner's real life counterpart may strike you as aloof and reserved. This characteristic is not uncommon among those governed by emotions and intuition. Seek him out and engage him. The Sojourner is keen to help you navigate the rocky terrain of emotional challenges.

THE WATCHER

Traditional Name: QUEEN of CUPS
QUEEN of MIRRORS
Attributes: CONTEMPLATIVE
INTUITIVE
Role: MYSTIC

The Watcher is a kind lady regarded by those who know her as a psychic or mystic. She might even be the person interpreting your Chrysalis Tarot reading. Her role as a mentor helps you develop you own psychic and intuitive abilities.

Marie Laveau, the Voodoo Queen of New Orleans, was a famous watcher from American history. Uncannily wise and always available to help others in times of need, she asks you to emulate her qualities and nurture your mystical talents and interests.

THE DREAMER

Traditional Name: KNIGHT of CUPS
KNIGHT of MIRRORS
Attributes: CONFIDENT
PASSIONATE
Role: MESSENGER

The Dreamer symbolizes mystical experience, so may not represent a real-life person. But if he is real, you'll recognize this passionate messenger straight away. His energy, symbolized by the leaping tiger, is boundless. His charm brims with hopefulness and desire to dream the impossible dream.

The Dreamer drifts effortlessly over land and sea upon carpets of romantic magic. He inspires you to sail the seas of your own imagination. Thoughts and dreams represent energy the Dreamer channels into real-life experiences.

THE HEALER

Traditional Name: PAGE of CUPS
PAGE of MIRRORS
Attributes: YOUTHFUL
SENSIBLE
Role: MUSE

The austere Mountain Pramnae were forest hermits who wore deerskin clothes bulging with curative herbs and roots to heal the sick. They were set apart as learned teachers and searchers of truth.

The Healer, when you meet her, will impress you with her practical demeanor. She likely will appear at a time when you need a strong, supportive shoulder. She'll inspire you to collect honey from the many blossoms of your experiences and turn it into a mystical balm of healing.

THE COMPANION

Traditional Name:	KING of WANDS
	KING of SPIRALS
Attributes:	VISIONARY
	ORGANIZER
Role:	MENTOR

The Companion turns positive intentions into reality. But be advised, he's a tad overbearing and impatient. Persistence aside, he lends good counsel with your best interests always at heart. The Companion's laughing kookaburra bird reminds him to lighten up.

If your goals seem illusive and you're banging your head against a wall, it's likely that an obstacle was placed in your path to change your thinking or slow your approach. Step back, discuss it with the Companion and commit to a course of action.

THE MUSE

Traditional Name: QUEEN of WANDS
QUEEN of SPIRALS
Attributes: NURTURING
INSPIRING
Role: MUSE

The Muse shares the qualities of a gentle fawn. She emerges from her magic forest in times of difficulty or indecision. The Muse can make herself known through a maternal presence or your inner voice—the stream of consciousness that knows you better than you know yourself.

The Muse brings comfort by assuring you of her concern and constancy. Like a guardian angel, she inspires the courage you need to make difficult choices.

THE CORSAIR

Traditional Name: KNIGHT of WANDS
KNIGHT of SPIRALS
Attributes: INDEPENDENT
STRONG-WILLED
Role: MYSTIC

The freedom-loving Corsair sails into your reading to shake it up a bit. Individuals with Corsair energy take great risks that yield substantial rewards. The treasures he most delights in plundering are cherished worldviews. He peers deeply into your subconscious to set it ablaze with mystical visions.

The Corsair is a man of action who inspires complete trust and confidence. His vibrant energy attracts enlightened spirits who feel and think as you do. The Corsair emboldens you to live life to the fullest on your own terms.

THE MIME

Traditional Name:	PAGE of WANDS
	PAGE of SPIRALS
Attributes:	INCISIVE
	MAGICAL
Role:	MESSENGER

The Mime is a wonderful card to have. You may recognize her impish real-life counterpart by her peculiar style of dress and carefree, droll personality. Recollecting fractured and repressed memories is the alchemical mission of the Mime.

The Otherworld places the Mime in your journey to soothe your psyche. Like a ram, she batters loose the memories of past experiences and returns them to mindfulness. The Mime then provides support to reconcile these memories through compassionate listening and sound advice.

THE POET

Traditional Name: KING of SWORDS
KNIGHT of SCROLLS
Attributes: INTELLECTUAL
LOGICAL
Role: MENTOR

Like a rabbit, the Poet thrives in the reality of the moment and in the subterranean depths of the subconscious mind. Be alert for a poet-type individual when you see this card. Scroll Troupe members all represent exceptionally evolved, emotionally balanced individuals, so it's important to establish your own interior balance. Then, you will attract personalities like the Poet into your life.

THE WEAVER

Traditional Name: QUEEN of SWORDS
QUEEN of SCROLLS
Attributes: DIPLOMATIC
TRANQUIL
Role: MUSE

In Greek mythology, Clotho, youngest of the Three Fates, wove the threads of life. This thread called *sutra* symbolizes cosmic connectivity, and with it the Weaver connects your life to your destiny. Like her Scroll colleagues, the

Weaver symbolizes the highest state of human consciousness. She sees the world in the spaces between light and darkness, clarity and confusion, fear and determination. The Weaver vibrates with the violet energy of the Otherworld. She helps you sort out life's chaotic trials and tribulations.

THE VISIONARY

Traditional Name:	KNIGHT of SWORDS
	KNIGHT of SCROLLS
Attributes:	HEALER
	TRAVELER
Role:	MYSTIC

With his exotic rattle and joyful mynah bird, the Visionary is the Troupe's spiritual healer. He resolves conflicting energies that confuse or misguide you. He helps you acquire patience as you await good things from beyond new horizons.

New beginnings offer abundant possibilities yet it's important to progress deliberately, step-by-step, pursuing pathways of light with a clear and open mind. How do you discover pathways of light? Eat wisely, meditate frequently and love unselfishly! The Visionary helps you appreciate life holistically.

THE PILGRIM

Traditional Name: PAGE of SWORDS
PAGE of SCROLLS
Attributes: PERSEVERANCE
ENDURANCE
Role: MESSENGER

The Pilgrim's llama symbolizes inner peace that comes from waving goodbye to creature comforts and the security of home, at least for a while. The distance a pilgrim travels matters not; the essence of the pilgrim's true journey is interior self-discovery.

The Pilgrim attains ascendancy through spiritual transformation and self-fulfillment. When you leave the castle behind to pursue the exotic butterfly, this card foretells positive changes taking place in your life.

```
        1               2



            SIGNIFICATOR
               CARD

  5                         3



            4
```

PENTAGRAM
FIVE-CARD SPREAD

We begin the reading by choosing a card to be the significator—the card that signifies you or the person for whom the reading is being done. We suggest beginning your Chrysalis Tarot experience by using the Storyteller card as your significator. She's card 9 in the Major Arcana. Feel free to choose a different card if another speaks to you. The significator card is placed face up in the center of the pentagram. The deck is then shuffled and cut three times. Five cards are selected and positioned facedown according to the diagram. The first card represents Spirit, the creative energy of your reading. The second symbolizes the element Earth, successively followed by Water, Fire and Air in that order. The cards are turned face up and read in the following sequence:

1 – SPIRIT
Represents the energy or impetus that guides your reading.

2 – EARTH
Symbolizes the present situation and your expectations.

3 – WATER
Symbolizes unexpected personal energies at play.

4 – FIRE
Symbolizes changes in the immediate future.

5 – AIR
Symbolizes the long-term outcome.

For our complete line of tarot decks, books, meditation cards, oracle sets, and other inspirational products please visit our website:

www.usgamesinc.com

Visit us on Facebook

U.S. GAMES SYSTEMS, INC.
179 Ludlow Street
Stamford, CT 06902 USA
203-353-8400
Order Desk 800-544-2637
FAX 203-353-8431